Susan B. Anthony

by Jill C. Wheeler

Published by ABDO & Daughters, an imprint of ABDO
Publishing Company, 4940 Viking Drive, Suite 622, Edina,
Minnesota 55435. Copyright ©2003 by Abdo Consulting
Group, Inc. International copyrights reserved in all countries.
No part of this book may be reproduced in any form without
written permission from the publisher.

Printed in the United States.

Edited by Paul Joseph
Graphic Design: John Hamilton
Cover Design: Mighty Media
Interior Photos: AP/Photo, p. 5, 6, 35, 38
Corbis, p. 1, 9, 11, 13, 15, 17, 18, 21, 22, 25, 27, 29, 31, 33, 37,
41, 43, 47, 49, 51, 55, 57, 59, 61

Library of Congress Cataloging-in-Publication Data

Wheeler, Jill C., 1964-
    Susan B. Anthony / Jill C. Wheeler.
        p. cm. — (Breaking barriers)
    Summary: Describes the life of the nineteenth-century crusader
who spent much of her life involved in the temperance, abolitionist,
and women's rights movements.
    Includes bibliographical references and index.
    ISBN 1-57765-903-1
    1. Anthony, Susan B. (Susan Brownell), 1820-1906—Juvenile
literature. 2. Feminists—United States—Biography—Juvenile
literature. 3. Suffragists—United States—Biography—Juvenile
literature. [1. Anthony, Susan B. (Susan Brownell), 1820-1906.
2. Suffragists. 3. Women—Biography.] I. Title.

HQ1413.A55 W5 2003
305.42'092—dc21
[B]

2002028199

Contents

A Time to Remember

In 1995, women around the United States celebrated the seventy-fifth anniversary of the Nineteenth Amendment. This amendment gave American women the right to vote. In California, the Votes for Women exhibit marked the anniversary of this historic law.

The exhibit featured writings, poetry, pictures, and songs that chronicled the suffrage movement. Many who saw the exhibit were surprised. They learned that the women's suffrage movement began in 1848. They also learned that suffragettes were often ridiculed, sometimes arrested, and frequently fired. The exhibit told these women's stories.

The exhibit also told of the brave women who dedicated their lives to securing the right to vote and fighting for equal rights for all American women. One of these women was Susan B. Anthony. Susan B., as she became known, spent her life working for human rights for all, especially women.

Susan B. Anthony

Susan B. Anthony

Anthony was an educated, unmarried political activist in an era when most women were none of these things. When Anthony was young, married women were more like slaves than citizens. They couldn't vote, enter into contracts, or buy or sell property in their name. They couldn't get a divorce unless their husband asked for it, or be guardians of their own children. Women were little more than possessions.

Anthony did not believe women should be treated as second-class citizens. A tireless worker, Anthony rose to become one of the best-known people of the century. She was sought after as a speaker and was invited to the White House many times. Perhaps more than any other woman in history, Susan B. Anthony is responsible for many of the rights and freedoms American women enjoy today.

A Bright Child

Susan Brownell Anthony was born on February 15, 1820, in Adams, Massachusetts. She was the second-oldest of eight children born to Daniel and Lucy Read Anthony. Only six of the Anthony children lived past infancy. Susan B.'s sisters were named Guelma, Hannah, and Mary. Daniel and Jacob Merritt were her brothers.

The Anthony family belonged to the Quaker religion. Quakers are a Christian group. They believe that anyone can feel and understand the word of God. Quakers believe ministers are not necessary to interpret God's word. They also believe that men and women are equal in the eyes of God.

Susan B.'s parents knew each other all their lives. As children, they often played together. Daniel left Adams as a young man to get an education. He later returned home to teach. Then Daniel fell in love with one of his students. Lucy was a lively, young farm girl. She loved to sing, dance, and wear pretty clothes. But Lucy was not a Quaker.

This portrait of Susan B. Anthony seated at her desk was taken around 1885.

Lucy lived much differently from the Quakers. Quakers frown upon singing and dancing. They also believe it is better to wear plain clothes. Most importantly, Quakers believe in only marrying other Quakers. Daniel and Lucy married anyway in 1817. Lucy made many sacrifices for the marriage. She had to change her lifestyle to that of the Quakers, even though she never became one.

Daniel soon went into business to support his family. He built a small mill to produce cotton cloth. Most of the workers in Daniel's mill were young women. Mill work was one of the few job options open to women of that day. Some others were teaching, cooking, cleaning, and doing chores as a hired girl.

Many of the mill workers lived with the Anthony family. Lucy had to work long, hard days just to take care of all of them. Susan B. and the other children helped as much as they could. Even at a young age, they were busy helping to feed and clothe the family and the mill workers.

Susan B. quickly proved herself a smart child. She learned her alphabet and could read and write by the time she was four years old. Her grandmothers encouraged her learning. So did her parents, who felt education was important for girls as well as boys.

Women working at a turn-of-the-century cotton mill.

An Early Education

When Susan B. was six, Daniel moved the family to Battenville, New York. Daniel had become a partner in a large cotton mill there. The Anthony children attended the local school.

Susan B. liked school but soon became frustrated. She especially wanted to learn long division. Her male teacher told her she could not learn it because she was a girl. So Susan B. persuaded a local farm boy to teach her long division. Later, she told her father about the teacher's failure to properly educate girls.

In those days, few people believed girls should be educated. But Susan B.'s father believed in educating both girls and boys. The Anthony family's new brick house included a one-room school. Daniel had built the school and hired a teacher because he wanted the best education for his children. He also opened the school to some of the local children. There, girls received the same education as the boys.

Susan B. Anthony

But Susan B. soon learned that inequality existed outside the classroom, too. When she was 11, one of the workers in her father's mill was sick and could not work. Both Susan B. and her younger sister Hannah asked if they could fill in. Daniel said one of them could work, and they would split the money. The two girls drew straws. Susan B. won, so she spent two weeks working at the mill. In return, she received $3.

Susan B. split her earnings with Hannah. Then she used her $1.50 to buy her mother a set of six blue cups. Susan B. didn't question keeping her half of the earnings. It seemed only fair, until she realized that few women at that time could keep their own money. The law in those days said that any money a woman earned belonged to her husband or male next of kin. It didn't matter if the man hadn't earned it.

Susan B. wasn't the only Anthony girl to earn her own money. She, Guelma, and Hannah began teaching when they were only 15 years old. They taught the children that attended the Anthony's home school.

Some people in Battenville criticized Daniel for letting his daughters work. They didn't think it was right for women to have jobs and earn money. They believed women should get married, stay home, and raise babies. Daniel ignored them. He believed in the Quaker doctrine that all people were equal in the eyes of God. He thought it was important for his daughters to experience independence.

A young girl watched by a supervisor pauses in her work at a cotton mill.

Reversal of Fortune

Susan B. switched from student to teacher when she was 15 years old. She spent summers teaching in her father's school. Then she taught the children of a family in a neighboring town. In the fall of 1837, she went back to school herself.

In 1837, women had few options for higher education. Only one college in the nation admitted women. However, some boarding schools did allow young women to take advanced courses. Susan B. went to a Quaker school near Philadelphia, Pennsylvania, that Guelma was attending. It was called Deborah Moulson's Female Seminary.

Susan B. was very homesick at first. She and her father, mother, and siblings were a very close family. Now she was nearly 300 miles (483 km) from home. To make matters worse, Susan B. got off to a bad start with the school's headmistress.

Deborah Moulson was in charge of the school, and she was very strict. She felt Susan B. didn't study enough. It seemed Susan B. could never please Moulson. Once, Moulson even complained that Susan B. didn't dot her i's the right way!

A female seminary in Keokuk, Iowa.

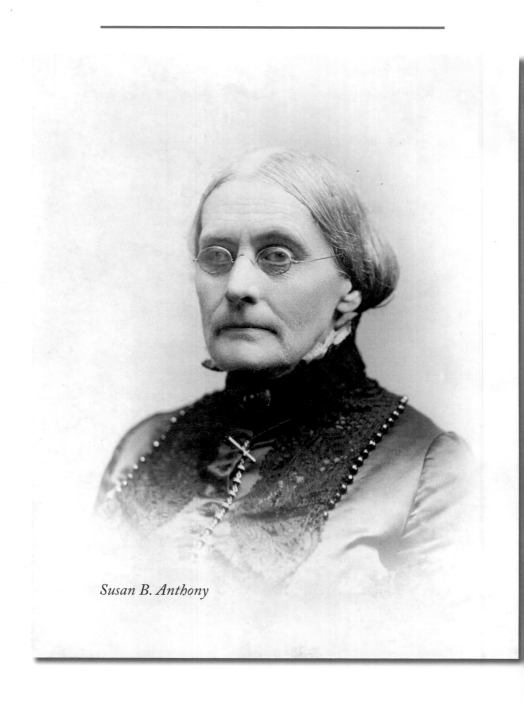

Susan B. Anthony

Everything changed in 1838. Susan B. and Guelma had to return to Battenville. The U.S. economy had tumbled into a major depression. Daniel lost his businesses and nearly all of his money. The Anthonys could no longer afford the $125-a-year tuition at the school. So Susan B. took a job teaching in a nearby town. This time she taught out of necessity rather than for fun.

The collapse of Daniel's businesses left the Anthony family with many debts. Their brick home and all their possessions had to be sold to pay them. It didn't matter that many of the things in the house belonged to Lucy. As a married woman, Lucy could not own any property. So all of her belongings were considered Daniel's. Therefore, everything was sold to help pay Daniel's debts.

Susan B. was shocked to see the contents of the house being sold. She was able to buy back a few things with money she had saved from her tiny teaching salary. Her mother's brother also helped buy back some of the Anthony's possessions. Susan B. never forgot the unfairness of the situation.

Better Single than Married

After the sale of their Battenville home, the family moved to nearby Hardscrabble, New York. With Daniel's help the town changed its name to Center Falls. Despite the loss of its money, the Anthony family remained rich with friends. Anthony and her sisters never lacked invitations to parties, buggy rides, and picnics.

Anthony never lacked boyfriends, either. The smart young woman with a mind of her own captivated many men. Anthony had a number of marriage proposals as a young woman. She turned them all down. "I was never engaged," she said. "Though I never said I would not marry. Simply this, I never found the man who was necessary to my happiness."

Anthony was later married to her cause, but she said if she had found the right man she would have wed. She said, "When a man says to me, 'Let us work together in the great cause you have undertaken'... I shall say 'I am yours truly' but he must ask me to be his equal, not his slave."

Susan B. Anthony

Susan B. Anthony on the doorstep of her home.

Anthony didn't hate men, as some reporters said. She did not blame them all for the inequality of women, either. Anthony respected any man that was fair and understood that women were also people. However, Anthony didn't know many men like that.

Anthony saw inequality in the marriages around her. She visited her cousin Margaret, who had recently had her fourth child. Margaret was lying very sick in bed when her husband complained of a headache. Margaret said she, too, had a headache, and it had stayed for two solid weeks. Her husband replied that his headache was truly painful and that his wife's was just a "sort of natural consequence." A few weeks later, Margaret died.

Anthony also saw inequality in her sister Guelma's marriage. Anthony had made a batch of biscuits to share with Guelma and Guelma's husband, Aaron. While they ate, Anthony mentioned that she was learning algebra. Aaron felt women should perform domestic duties and men should be educated. He said, "I'd rather see a woman make biscuits like these than solve the knottiest problem in algebra." Anthony replied without missing a beat, "There is no reason why she should not be able to do both."

The "Smartest" Woman

Anthony spent some time with her family in Center Falls. Then in 1839, she took a teaching job in New Rochelle, New York. She sent all of her money home to help support her family. Later that year, she returned to Center Falls to take another teaching position. She replaced a male teacher who had been fired for not doing his job. The male teacher had earned $10 a week. Anthony was paid $2.50 a week for doing the exact same job.

Daniel was never able to get back on track financially. In 1845, he decided to try his hand at farming. Lucy's inheritance helped him buy a farm near Rochester, New York. Anthony, her mother, and her younger siblings moved with him.

The Rochester Quaker community welcomed the Anthonys. Almost immediately they were swept up into the big discussions of the day. Quakers opposed drinking alcohol. They felt drinking led to alcoholism. People who suffered from alcoholism frequently abused or neglected their families. Some people actively tried to get alcohol outlawed. Their fight was called the temperance movement.

Susan B. Anthony

In addition to temperance, the Quakers often discussed slavery. Some Quaker people felt slavery was wrong. They believed that all slaves should be freed. People who believed slavery should end were called abolitionists.

The Anthony family began to host weekly meetings at their home to talk about these issues. Anthony enjoyed the discussions at the meetings. She became convinced that slavery was wrong. She began to read William Lloyd Garrison's newspaper, *The Liberator*. The newspaper encouraged people to work to end slavery.

In 1846, when Anthony was 26, she left Rochester to take a new job. She became headmistress of the female students at Canajoharie Academy. The academy was located in Canajoharie, New York. Anthony excelled at her teaching job. People were surprised by the new headmistress. Some called her "the smartest woman who ever came to Canajoharie."

While there, she lived with a cousin from her mother's side of the family. Her cousin's family was not Quaker, so their lifestyle was different from what Anthony was used to. Anthony enjoyed the change. She began to shed her plain, gray dresses in exchange for brighter, more stylish ones.

After three years of teaching, Anthony reached a crossroads. She was just 29 years old but was already earning the top salary for a female teacher. Plus, there was little challenge left for her in being a teacher. She wanted to do something new. She just didn't know what that was. She returned to Rochester in 1849 to plan her next move.

Susan B. Anthony working at her desk.

An Activist is Born

The first woman's rights convention was held at Seneca Falls, New York, in 1848. Daniel, Lucy, and Mary Anthony attended the second woman's rights convention in Rochester a few months later. The Anthonys were excited about the ideas presented at the convention. They even signed a list of resolutions demanding equal rights for women.

Anthony had not attended either convention. Yet she kept hearing about the issue of women's rights when she returned to her family's farm. She also heard more about the temperance movement and the abolitionist movement. The Anthony family regularly entertained such activists as William Lloyd Garrison and Frederick Douglass.

Anthony embraced these causes with her family. She made her first speech in favor of temperance. Anthony joined the Rochester chapter of the Daughters of Temperance. It was a women's group dedicated to getting people to stop drinking alcohol. It was also Anthony's opportunity to begin public speaking.

Susan B. Anthony was portrayed as a stern activist in this editorial cartoon.

Anthony became an activist. In those days, that meant making speeches. There were no televisions or radios then. People stayed informed by reading newspapers or by attending lectures. They would drive for miles to hear someone speak on an issue. Lectures were a popular form of entertainment.

Early in her career, Anthony attended a Sons of Temperance meeting in Albany, New York. She tried to speak during the convention, but the men there silenced her. "The sisters were not invited here to speak, but to listen and learn," they said.

Anthony was angry and frustrated. She had spoken in front of women's groups before. And she had seen women address Quaker meetings of men and women many times. Anthony thought there was nothing wrong with a woman addressing a group of both men and women.

Anthony had another bad experience at a state teacher's convention. The men were debating why teaching was not a respected profession. Once again, she tried to speak. The men silenced her, even though most of the teachers there were women.

Anthony insisted on speaking. The men debated for 30 minutes before allowing her to speak. Anthony said, "Do you not see that so long as society says woman has not brains enough to be a doctor, lawyer, or minister, but has plenty to be a teacher, every man of you, who condescends to teach admits… that he has no more brains than a woman?"

The meeting broke up shortly after her comments. Three men congratulated Anthony for her remarks, but many people disapproved of her speaking. Even some women felt it was wrong and deliberately avoided Anthony. Others praised her for her courage.

Women perform an open-air prayer meeting in front of a saloon in Springfield, Ohio, in 1874.

The Cause Begins

Anthony's life changed once again in May 1851. She traveled to Seneca Falls, New York, to hear William Lloyd Garrison speak. While there, Amelia Bloomer introduced her to Elizabeth Cady Stanton.

Stanton had already been fighting for women's rights for years. She and Anthony liked each other right away. Yet Stanton felt women's rights was the top issue of the day. Anthony disagreed. She still felt she should focus her efforts on temperance.

It wasn't until 1853 that Anthony agreed with Stanton. Anthony realized that women needed to have equal rights in order to enact reform. That included temperance. Anthony began to concentrate on equal rights for everyone. She believed men and women, black and white, should all have equal rights. Above all, she dedicated her energy to winning voting rights for women.

Elizabeth Cady Stanton with her daughter Harriet in 1856.

Anthony felt, to make a difference in other issues, women first had to have more legal rights. In the 1800s, women did not have the power to change unfair laws regarding property ownership or equal pay for equal work. Anthony felt the only way to gain this power was through voting. First, she had to educate the people about the suffrage issue. She worked with Stanton to do this.

Anthony and Stanton made a strange couple. Anthony was unmarried with no children. She had the time and energy to crisscross the state and, later, the nation. She was a natural at organizing people and things. Likewise, her speaking abilities were powerful.

Anthony was rarely at a loss for words when her arguments were challenged. Her quick wit and sharp intellect impressed many critics. Once, an abolitionist speaker challenged her about speaking out on the subject of marriage. "You are not married," he said. "You have no business to be discussing marriage." Anthony quickly replied, "You are not a slave, suppose you quit lecturing on slavery."

Stanton, meanwhile, had a husband and seven children. She couldn't always leave her family to go fight for the cause. However, she wrote brilliant speeches that Anthony could deliver. Stanton often supplied the words. Anthony supplied the passion.

"We have made arguments that have stood unshaken through the storms of long years," Stanton said of the partnership, "Arguments that no one has answered."

In addition to speaking and lecturing, women's rights activists also used petitions to spread the suffrage movement. In 1854, Anthony and her supporters went door-to-door gathering signatures on a petition. The petition asked the New York State Legislature to allow married women to keep the money they earned. Anthony's group gathered 6,000 signatures. Despite all the signatures, the legislature refused to change the law.

Susan B. Anthony, left, and Elizabeth Cady Stanton sit on the porch of Anthony's house in Rochester, New York.

The Roots of Inequality

Anthony was 33 years old when she decided to focus her attention on women's suffrage. She would spend more than 50 years tirelessly working on winning the right for women to vote.

It is hard for many people today to understand Anthony's struggle. Yet she and others in the women's movement had to change minds person by person. Even many women were hard to convince. Anthony had the door slammed in her face by women many times. Many feared change. Others didn't realize how much better their lives could be if things did change.

Anthony encountered other powerful forces against change, too. Many of the problems reformers had in abolishing slavery and getting equal rights for women had the same roots. Those roots were in business and religion.

Christian preachers claimed the Bible said black people and women were inferior to white men. Therefore, it was acceptable to hold African-Americans as slaves. And women could be restricted to the home, mill, or schoolroom.

Susan B. Anthony

This bronze sculpture of chained slaves by Bernard Jackson shows how slaves were transported in shackles aboard slave ships.

Many businesspeople also had reasons for supporting slavery and the inequality of women. Textile industries relied on cotton produced by slaves. While these businesspeople may not have approved of slavery, they realized it was helping them make money.

Likewise, the alcohol industry opposed women's suffrage. Many women believed in the temperance movement. If women could vote, the businesspeople believed alcohol would be outlawed. The alcohol industry gave lots of money to fight women's suffrage.

Because of these forces, Anthony and her supporters were virtually powerless. Their opponents had money, power, and votes. They had none. All Anthony had were her convictions, her brain, and her family's support. She needed all to survive the threats, ridicule, and personal attacks she faced each day.

One Step Forward, Two Steps Back

Anthony and Stanton realized one victory in 1860. The New York State Legislature finally allowed women to keep the money they earned, share guardianship of their children, and keep property if widowed. That battle alone had taken six years of hard work.

Meanwhile, lawmakers debated the topic of slavery in the United States for years. As the 1860s began, the new U.S. territories in the West made it a prominent issue. Territories such as Kansas were able to decide whether they would be slaveholding states. Pro- and anti-slave groups each sent people to Kansas to try to swing the vote in their favor.

Anthony had been against slavery and racism since she was a child. She had been appalled once when she saw racism at a Quaker meeting. Here were people who said they opposed slavery. Yet they didn't want a black man to worship with them! Anthony could not tolerate such hypocrisy.

Susan B. Anthony, standing, looks over the shoulder of Elizabeth Cady Stanton.

As the slavery debate grew, Anthony and her family left the Quaker Church. They joined the Unitarian Church instead. The Unitarians called for immediate abolition of slavery.

Anthony believed equal rights for all meant rights for women and slaves. She had often spoken out against slavery. She even assisted her friend Harriet Tubman, a conductor on the Underground Railroad, to help slaves escape. Anthony increased her anti-slavery efforts as the American Civil War loomed.

Her speeches were not popular. Pro-slavery people heckled her. They threw rotten eggs at her. Once they made a dummy and labeled it Susan B. Anthony. They dragged the dummy through the streets, then burned it. Another time the mayor of Albany, New York, had to sit on the platform with her while she spoke. He held a loaded pistol in his lap to keep the peace.

The American Civil War began in 1861. In 1862, Anthony's father died. Anthony was heartbroken. "It seemed to me the world and everybody in it must stop," she said of his death. Yet she pressed on with her cause. In 1863, President Abraham Lincoln freed the slaves in the Confederate States when he issued the Emancipation Proclamation.

Harriet Tubman was an escaped slave who later became a leader of the Underground Railroad, helping other slaves gain their freedom.

This illustration, entitled The First Vote, *by A.R. Waud, shows African-Americans going to the polls for the first state elections in the South after the Civil War.*

Anthony and other abolitionists felt this was not enough. They wanted a constitutional amendment outlawing slavery. Anthony began a petition drive. By 1864, they had collected 400,000 signatures. It was an amazing accomplishment. Shortly after that, the U.S. Senate passed the Thirteenth Amendment, which outlawed slavery.

Anthony's joy did not last long. After the Civil War ended, talk began about a constitutional amendment granting African-Americans the right to vote. Anthony learned that the proposed language gave the vote only to male citizens.

Anthony and other women suffragists pressed hard for the word *male* to be taken out of the amendment. Yet even some of her abolitionist and suffragist friends disagreed. They told her it was the black man's turn for suffrage. Forcing an approval of voting rights for blacks and women might mean no amendment at all. Women, they said, would have to wait.

The Revolution

Frustrated, Anthony worked even harder than before on women's rights. Petitions weren't enough, she realized. Unless the people who signed the petitions also voted, Congressmen wouldn't pay attention to them.

To show why she felt this way, Anthony told this story: "In New York we got up a petition signed by over 2,800. It was presented to the Legislature. It was read and laughed at and laid on the table. A young man... said: 'Who are these people that have signed the petition? Nothing but women and children.' It fell to the floor and he kicked it.... I then resolved to use my life to make women as good as men."

Anthony traveled thousands of miles in all types of weather. Sometimes she spoke to large crowds in town halls. Other times she had to struggle to find a place to speak. But she spoke wherever she could, even in schoolhouses, barns, sawmills, and cabins. Anywhere she could, she spread the word for suffrage.

The Revolution.

PRINCIPLE, NOT POLICY: JUSTICE, NOT FAVORS.

VOL. I.—NO. 1.   NEW YORK, WEDNESDAY, JANUARY 8, 1868. $2.00 A YEAR.

The Revolution;

THE ORGAN OF THE

NATIONAL PARTY OF NEW AMERICA.

PRINCIPLE, NOT POLICY—INDIVIDUAL RIGHTS AND RESPONSIBILITIES.

THE REVOLUTION WILL ADVOCATE:

1. IN POLITICS—Educated Suffrage, Irrespective of Sex or Color; Equal Pay to Women for Equal Work; Eight Hours Labor; Abolition of Standing Armies and Part. Despotisms. Down with Politicians—Up with the People!

2. IN RELIGION—Deeper Thought; Broader Idea; Science not Superstition; Personal Purity; Love to Man as well as God.

3. IN SOCIAL LIFE—Morality and Reform; Practical Education, not Theoretical; Facts not Fiction; Virtue not Vice; Cold Water not Alcoholic Drinks or Medicines. It will indulge in no Gross Personalities and insort no Quack or Immoral Advertisements, as common even in Religious Newspapers.

4. THE REVOLUTION proposes a new Commercial and Financial Policy. America no longer led by Europe. Gold like our Cotton and Corn for sale. Greenbacks for money. An American System of Finance. American Products and Labor Free. Foreign Manufactures Prohibited. Open doors to Artisans and Immigrants. Atlantic and Pacific Oceans for American Steamships and Shipping; or American goods in American bottoms. New York the Financial Centre of the World. Wall Street emancipated from Bank of England, or American Cash for American Bills. The Credit Foncier and Credit Mobilier System, or Capital Mobilized to Resuscitate the South and our Mining Interests, and to People the Country from Ocean to Ocean, from Omaha to San Francisco. More organized Labor, more Cotton, more Gold and Silver Bullion to sell foreigners at the highest prices. Ten millions of Naturalized Citizens DEMAND A PENNY OCEAN POSTAGE, to Strengthen the Brotherhood of Labor; and if Congress Vote One Hundred and Twenty-five Millions for a Standing Army and Freedman's Bureau, cannot they spare One Million to Educate Europe and to keep bright the chain of acquaintance and friendship between those millions and their fatherland?

Send in your Subscription. THE REVOLUTION, published weekly, will be the Great Organ of the Age.

TERMS.—Two dollars a year, in advance. Ten names ($20) entitle the sender to one copy free.

ELIZABETH CADY STANTON, | EDS.
PARKER PILLSBURY, |

SUSAN B. ANTHONY,
Proprietor and Manager.
37 Park Row (Room 17), New York City.
To whom address all business letters.

KANSAS.

THE question of the enfranchisement of woman has already passed the court of moral discussion, and is now fairly ushered into the arena of politics, where it must remain a fixed element of debate, until party necessity shall compel its success.

With 9,000 votes in Kansas, one-third the entire vote, every politician must see that the friends of "woman's suffrage" hold the balance of power in that State to-day. And those 9,000 votes represent a principle deep in the hearts of the people, for this triumph was secured without money, without a press, without a party. With these instrumentalities now fast coming to us on all sides, the victory in Kansas is but the herald of greater victories in every State of the Union. Kansas already leads the world in her legislation for woman on questions of property, education, wages, marriage and divorce. Her best universities are open alike to boys and girls. In fact woman has a voice in the legislation of that State. She votes on all school questions and is eligible to the office of trustee. She has a voice in temperance too; no license is granted without the consent of a majority of the adult citizens, male and female, black and white. The consequence is, some school houses are voted up in every part of the State, and rum voted down. Many of the ablest men in that State are champions of woman's cause. Governors, judges, lawyers and clergymen. Two-thirds of the press and pulpits advocate the idea, in spite of the opposition of politicians. The first Governor of Kansas, twice chosen to that office, Charles Robinson, went all through the State, speaking every day for two months in favor of woman suffrage. In the organization of the State government, he proposed that the words "white male" should not be inserted in the Kansas constitution. All this shows that giving political rights to women is no new idea in that State. Who that has listened with tearful eyes to the deep experiences of those Kansas women, through the darkest hours of their history, does not feel that such bravery and self denial as they have shown alike in war and peace, have richly earned for them the crown of citizenship.

Opposed to this moral sentiment of the liberal minds of the State, many adverse influences were brought to bear through the entire campaign.

The action of the New York Constitutional Convention; the silence of eastern journals on the question; the opposition of abolitionists lost a demand for woman's suffrage should defeat negro suffrage; the hostility everywhere of black men themselves; some even stumping the State against woman's suffrage; the official action of both the leading parties in their conventions in Leavensworth against the proposition, with every organized Republican influ-

ence outside as well as inside the State, all combined might have made our vote comparatively a small one, had not George Francis Train gone into the State two weeks before the election and galvanized the Democrats into their duty, thus securing 9,000 votes for woman's suffrage. Some claim that we are indebted to the Republicans for this vote; but the fact that the most radical republican district, Douglass County, gave the largest vote against woman's suffrage, while Leavenworth, the Democratic district, gave the largest vote for it, fully belies that question.

In saying that Mr. Train helped to swell our vote takes nothing from the credit due all those who labored faithfully for months in that State. All praise to Olympia Brown, Lucy Stone, S——B. Anthony, Henry B. Blackwell, and ——ge Wood, who welcomed, for an idea, the hardships of travelling in a new State, fording streams, scaling rocky brinks, sleeping on the ground and eating hard tack, with the fatigue of constant speaking, in school-houses, barns, mills, depots and the open air; and especially, all praise to the glorious Hutchinson family—John, his son Henry and daughter, Viola—who, with their own horses and carriage, made the entire circuit of the state, singing Woman's Suffrage into souls that logic could never penetrate. Having shared with them the hardships, with them I rejoice in our success.

E. C. S.

THE BALLOT—BREAD, VIRTUE, POWER.

THE REVOLUTION will contain a series of articles, beginning next week, to prove the power of the ballot in elevating the character and condition of woman. We shall show that the ballot will secure for woman equal place and equal wages in the world of work; that it will open to her the schools, colleges, professions and all the opportunities and advantages of life; that in her hand it will be a moral power to stay the tide of vice and crime and misery on every side. In the words of Bishop Simpson—

"We believe that the great vices in our large cities will never be conquered until the ballot is put in the hands of women. If the question of the danger of these sons being drawn away into drinking saloons was brought up, if the mothers had the power, they would close them; if the sisters had the power, and they saw their brothers going away to haunts of infamy, they would close those places. You may get men to trifle with purity, with virtue, with righteousness; but, thank God, the hearts of the women of our land—the mothers, wives and daughters—are too pure to wink at a compromise either with intemperance or licentiousness."

Thus, too, shall we purge our constitutions and statute laws from all invidious distinctions among the citizens of the States, and secure the same civil and moral code for man and woman. We will show the hundred thousand female teachers, and the millions of laboring women, that their complaints, petitions, strikes and protective unions are of no avail until they hold the ballot in their own hands; for it is the first step toward social, religious and political equality.

As Anthony traveled and spoke, she quickly learned to put her main points in tight sentences. This way, she could get her message out quickly. Today, people call these tightly worded sentences sound bites.

Anthony usually traveled alone. For a woman, that was nearly unheard of. Often her reception in new places was hostile. She spent many nights in cold, dirty rooms. It was a hard life on the road, and often very lonely.

Anthony, Stanton, and other women's rights activists founded the American Equal Rights Association (AERA) to fight for universal suffrage. On a trip to Kansas, Anthony met a wealthy businessman named George Francis Train. Train believed in the rights Anthony and Stanton sought for women. He offered to give them money to start a newspaper.

Anthony and Stanton accepted Train's offer and created *The Revolution*. Anthony employed women to typeset the newspaper. Besides women's suffrage, the paper addressed many other controversial issues. It addressed the issue of equal pay for women. It also promoted labor unions in order to get better wages and working conditions.

Train left the United States shortly after promising Anthony money. He helped a little, but the newspaper's debts grew. The publication was well researched and well written. However, it was too controversial to attain a large readership. Sadly, Anthony sold the publication in 1870 for $1. She had published the newspaper for two years.

Anthony was left with $10,000 in debt, which she vowed to pay. She began to slowly pay off the debt. Anthony charged 25 cents per person to hear her speak. She sold women's rights literature as well. Six years later, Anthony paid it all back.

The last payment on the debt made headlines in many newspapers. Suddenly, even Anthony's critics respected her. One newspaper wrote that she paid her debts "like a man." At that time, it was the ultimate compliment.

Susan B. Anthony and Elizabeth Cady Stanton

Pressing the Question

Despite the work of the AERA, the Fourteenth Amendment passed. It was soon followed by the Fifteenth Amendment. That measure said U.S. citizens could vote regardless of "race, color, or previous condition of servitude."

In 1869, Anthony, Stanton, and other suffragettes formed the National Woman Suffrage Association (NWSA). For the next 21 years, the organization worked to get women the right to vote. Then the NWSA merged with another group to form the National-American Woman Suffrage Association (NAWSA). The NAWSA continued to work for another 30 years.

The Fourteenth and Fifteenth Amendments got Anthony and her supporters thinking. The Fourteenth Amendment gave citizenship and citizens' rights to "all persons born or naturalized in the United States." Therefore, they reasoned, all women who were citizens should have the right to vote.

Susan B. Anthony

Anthony and a number of other brave women decided to test this theory. They voted in the election of 1872. A few days later, Anthony, age 52, was arrested for her act. After her indictment, she was released on $1,000 bail. She spent the months between her arrest and trial traveling across New York, talking about the case. She was glad that she'd been arrested. It was helping her call further attention to women's suffrage.

Anthony's trial took place in June 1873. From the beginning, it was unfair. Judge Ward Hunt strongly opposed giving women the right to vote. Anthony was not allowed to speak in her own defense. That was because, as a woman, the law considered her incompetent. Anthony's lawyer, Henry Selden, argued her case instead.

After all the arguments, Judge Hunt reached into his pocket. Anthony watched in disbelief as he pulled out his statement. He had written it before any evidence had been presented! He then read his statement before the packed courtroom. The judge ordered the jury to find Anthony guilty. Then he dismissed them.

Anthony and Selden were shocked. Selden tried to protest. The judge silenced him. The jurors, likewise, were shocked. Even though all were white men, they had not been able to say a word.

Anthony got her chance to speak the next day before sentencing. The judge asked her if she had anything to say before he passed sentence. "Yes, your honor," she began. "I have many things to say." Anthony went on for several minutes, ignoring the judge's attempts to silence her. She talked about how her rights had been trampled, being denied a vote, and being denied a fair trial.

The judge grew angrier. Then he delivered the sentence. He fined Anthony $100 plus court costs. Anthony responded calmly, "May it please your honor, I shall never pay a dollar of your unjust penalty." Then she added, "I shall earnestly and persistently continue to urge all women… that 'Resistance to tyranny is obedience to God.' "

Anthony never did pay the fine. However, the judge never sent her to jail for disobeying. He deliberately let her go so she could not appeal her case to a higher court. Had she been able to appeal, the women's voting question might have gone to the United States Supreme Court.

In Search of an Amendment

Anthony had been arrested for voting. Another suffragette, Virginia Minor, sued when election officials refused to register her to vote. Her case did go to the Supreme Court. But it was a major disappointment. The Court said that the Constitution did guarantee rights to citizens. However, it said those rights would be defined by states, not the federal government.

Anthony and others in the movement knew they needed a women's suffrage amendment to the Constitution. A sixteenth amendment had been proposed in 1868. The NWSA collected 10,000 signatures, which the Senate ridiculed. In 1878, Elizabeth Cady Stanton revised the Sixteenth Amendment proposal. A California senator presented it to the Senate, at the urging of Anthony and the NWSA. The Senate defeated the amendment.

Susan B. Anthony and Elizabeth Cady Stanton

Anthony saw to it that the amendment was presented again the next year, and the next year, and the one after that. Every year, Anthony went to Washington, D.C., to plead the case of women's suffrage. Some people joked about seeing her trademark red shawl on Capitol Hill each year. They said it was a sure sign of spring. In fact, Anthony appeared before every U.S. Congress between 1869 and 1906.

Anthony's highly publicized trial thrust women's suffrage firmly into the headlines. It also forced people to think. Before, many people thought feminists were crazy. Slowly, feminists were earning more respect. Where Anthony had once been heckled, she began to be praised. "During those days," Anthony said, "people who did not know me thought I was a witch with horns. That has all passed and I am accorded nearly the same privileges as men in my country."

Newspapers often portrayed Anthony as a mean old maid. In reality, she was a warm person with a lively sense of humor. Pictures show her looking stern because of the era's photography. People had to hold their poses for so long that it was uncomfortable to smile. Yet most people concentrated on her personality rather than on her appearance.

Her hard-working personality also made Anthony a mentor. She inspired many young women to join the movement. They called her Aunt Susan. Anthony also traveled to Europe to meet with suffragettes there. She was instrumental in creating an international organization dedicated to women's rights. The International Council of Women held its first convention in 1888.

The movement realized a glimmer of success in 1890. Wyoming Territory had given women the right to vote in 1869. In 1890, Wyoming was to be admitted as a state. Congress insisted Wyoming limit the vote to men. Wyoming officials refused. "[We will] remain out of the Union a hundred years rather than come in without woman suffrage," they declared. This forced Congress to accept them on their terms. Wyoming became the first state where women could vote. Colorado, Idaho, and Utah followed.

Susan B. Anthony, seated center, and other members of the International Council of Women.

Failure is Impossible

Anthony was growing old and tired. In 1900, she retired as president of the NAWSA just before her eightieth birthday. She continued to travel and speak, though not as much. In 1902, Stanton died.

Anthony gave her last public speech at a suffrage convention in Washington, D.C. It was February 1906. "I am here for a little time only," she said. "The fight must not cease; you must see that it does not stop." She ended her speech with the simple words, "Failure is impossible."

Several weeks later, Anthony came down with pneumonia. She died at her home in Rochester, New York, on March 13, 1906.

Anthony never lived to see the amendment she had spent most of her life fighting to win. Yet she had trained a new generation of women's rights leaders. They marched on without her.

On August 26, 1920, the Nineteenth Amendment was ratified. It was called the Susan B. Anthony Amendment. It said voting rights could not be denied because of sex. U.S. women voted for the first time in the election of November 1920. One hundred years after her birth, Susan B. Anthony's dream had finally come true.

Susan B. Anthony

Timeline

February 15, 1820: Susan B. Anthony is born in Adams, Massachusetts.

1846: Anthony starts teaching at Canajoharie Academy.

1851: Anthony travels to Seneca Falls, New York, to attend anti-slavery convention. There, she meets Elizabeth Cady Stanton.

1863: Anthony and Stanton write the "Appeal to the Women of the Republic."

1868: Anthony begins publication of *The Revolution*, which calls for equal rights for women.

1872-1873: Anthony is arrested in Albany, New York, for voting. She is found guilty, but refuses to pay her fine. The judge frees her so she can't appeal the ruling.

March 13, 1906: Susan B. Anthony dies.

1920: The Nineteenth Amendment to the U.S. Constitution grants the right to vote to all women in the United States.

Web Sites

Would you like to learn more about Susan B. Anthony? Please visit **www.abdopub.com** to find up-to-date Web site links about Susan B. Anthony and the women's rights movement. These links are routinely monitored and updated to provide the most current information available.

The front and back of the Susan B. Anthony one-dollar coin.

Glossary

activist

A person who actively works for change, usually on a social cause.

boarding school

A school where students both study and live away from home.

Confederate States

The 11 slaveholding Southern states that seceded from the Union to form the Confederate States of America.

depression

A severe economic downturn.

draw straws

To decide something by having people select from a group of straws, of which one straw has been made shorter than the other. The person who draws the short one wins.

hypocrisy

To say one thing and then act differently.

Quaker

A member of the Religious Society of Friends, a Christian group.

secede

To withdraw from an organized political body, such as a nation.

suffrage

The right to vote.

suffragette

A woman who works for the right for women to vote.

suffragist

A person who works to help more people get the right to vote. Historically the term was used with people who worked to get the vote for women.

Underground Railroad

A network of people opposed to slavery who illegally helped fugitive slaves reach safety.

Unitarian Church

A religious group that stresses individual freedom of belief.

Index

QUESTIONNAIRE ON COLLABORATION: EVALUATION OF GROUP FUNCTIONING

The following questions are designed to gather information about the participation of other members of your group on [your current] project. Please respond to each honestly using the following scale. Try to think of the group as a whole. So, if some members behave in certain ways and other members do not, then respond to the question somewhere in the middle of the scale.

1 = not at all   2 = somewhat   3 = moderately   4 = very

TO WHAT EXTENT DO YOU BELIEVE OTHER MEMBERS:

1. Are familiar with the goals of this project?

   1   2   3   4

2. Accept the goals of this project?

   1   2   3   4

3. Feel responsible for carrying out the goals of this project?

   1   2   3   4

4. Have been assigned specific responsibilities to carry out the project?

   1   2   3   4

5. Understand what is expected of them?

   1   2   3   4

6. Understand the procedures necessary to complete the project?

   1   2   3   4

7. Listen to what other team members have to say?

   1   2   3   4

8. Feel free to express their feelings about an issue in the group?

   1   2   3   4

9. Express their feelings honestly about an issue in the group?

   1   2   3   4

10. Feel free to suggest ideas about the direction of the project?

   1   2   3   4

11. Feel free to disagree with each other about an idea?

   1   2   3   4

12. Offer support when other members make their ideas, feelings, or reactions known?

   1   2   3   4

13. Have confidence that other group members will complete assigned tasks?

   1   2   3   4

14. Volunteer for specific group tasks?

   1   2   3   4

15. Take responsibility for providing their expertise in group decisions?

   1   2   3   4

16. Value the opinions of other group members?

   1   2   3   4

17. Are willing to assume responsibility for making a decision for the group in areas where they have expertise?

    1   2   3   4

18. Participate in the group discussion?

    1   2   3   4

19. Look at the tasks of the team?

    1   2   3   4

20. Feel a real part of the team?

    1   2   3   4

21. Feel comfortable when differences of opinion are expressed or there is conflict?

    1   2   3   4

Index

Springer Publishing Company

APPLYING HEALTH SERVICES RESEARCH TO LONG-TERM CARE

James C. Romeis, PhD, Rodney M. Coe, PhD, John E. Morley, MB, BCh

This volume addresses the need for greater application of health research advances to the practice of caring for the elderly population. Based on their renowned geriatric research program, the expert editors demonstrate ways to promote and enhance quality in long-term care. Topics include increasing preventive care of the elderly, strengthening community-based services for caregiver support, and integrating acute care and long-term care services. For all long-term care professionals and health services providers for the elderly, and educators in these fields.

Contents:

1996   232pp   0-8261-9140-1   hardcover

536 Broadway, New York, NY 10012-3955 • (212) 431-4370 • Fax (212) 941-7842

Springer Publishing Company

EVALUATING YOUR PRACTICE
A Guide to Self-Assessment

Catherine F. Alter, PhD & Wayne Evens, MSW

This easily accessible text provides step-by-step guidelines for choosing and implementing self-assessment research. Featuring a wealth of case histories and examples, the book emphasizes data collection and analysis methods, and spans the three levels of social work practice: direct practice, administration and community organization.

> Springer Series on Social Work
>
> ## Evaluating Your Practice
> A Guide to Self-Assessment
> Catherine F. Alter
> Wayne Evens

Contents:

- Self-Assessment Research
- Designing Self-Assessments
- Analysis of Data
- Qualitative Designs
- Quantitative Designs
- Social Work Practice and Research
- Appendices: The Self-Assessment Checklist
- 100+ Outcome Measures
- Annotated Bibiliography of Books of Scales
- Microcomputer Software for Self-Assessments
- Creating Templates for Statistical Tests
- Human Subjects Review

Springer Series on Social Work
1990   208pp   0-8261-6960-0   hardcover

536 Broadway, New York, NY 10012-3955 • (212) 431-4370 • Fax (212) 941-7842

ⓢ *Springer Publishing Company*

PROGRAM EVALUATION IN THE HUMAN SERVICES
Michael J. Smith, DSW

"Smith has written an outstanding introductory program evaluation text for students of the human services. He effectively balances presentation of the major technical concepts in evaluation research with good advice about how program evaluation should be done. Particularly effective are the examples drawn from his personal experiences as an evaluation researcher."

—Francis G. Caro, PhD, *University of Massachusetts*

Contents:

- An Introduction to Program Evaluation
- A Comprehensive Definition of Program Evaluation
- The First Step: Describing the Program
- The Second Step: Defining the Program Goals
- The Third Step: Designing the Study
- The Fourth and Fifth Steps: Implementing the Program Evaluation
- The Sixth Step: Conclusions, Implications and Recommendations
- Appendices

Springer Series on Social Work
1990   168pp   0-8261-6590-7   hardcover

536 Broadway, New York, NY 10012-3955 • (212) 431-4370 • Fax (212) 941-7842

$P *Springer Publishing Company*

DILEMMAS IN HUMAN SERVICE MANAGEMENT
Illustrative Case Studies

Raymond Sanchez Mayers, PhD, **Federico Souflee, Jr.,** PhD, and **Dick J. Schoech,** PhD

The authors have combined their experience as teachers and social workers to create actual case studies, with discussion questions to help prepare students for real world problems. A broad range of situations are discussed—from sexual harassment to ethical concerns and management theory.

Partial Contents:

- Human Services Management in Perspective
- An Accounting Clerk for DSS
- Developing an Information System
- Breaking Up Is Hard To Do
- Which Side Are You On?
- The Battered Women's Shelter of Aiken County
- Planning and the Politics of Inclusion
- Staffing a Planning Committee
- The Politically Correct Candidate
- Whose Values: The Politics of Planning
- A Sexual Harassment Complaint
- Inertia on the Board
- The Price of Serving
- "Creative" Grant Writing for Survival
- Too Many Chiefs
- Staff Meetings at Senior Citizen Centers of the Valley, Inc.

Springer Series on Social Work
1994   184pp   0-8261-7740-9   hard

536 Broadway, New York, NY 10012-3955 • (212) 431-4370 • Fax (212) 941-7842